Scho

This book belongs to

FS109008 • School Skills

Round and Round

Color the circles.

Trace. Draw **2** more circles.

FS109008 • School Skills

One Is Different

Color the one that is different in each row.

Color two the same. Color one different.

FS109008 • School Skills

The Biggest of All

Color the biggest one in each row.

Draw a triangle that is bigger than the others.

 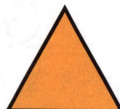

A Lot of Rectangles

Color the rectangles.

Trace. Draw **2** more rectangles.

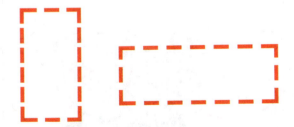

FS109008 • School Skills

I Want My Mommy!

Trace the line from each baby to its mother.

FS109008 • School Skills

Three Corners

Color the triangles.

Trace. Draw **2** more triangles.

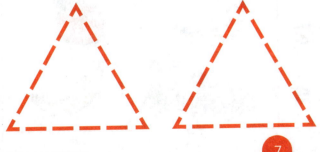

FS109008 • School Skills

Match Them Up

Draw lines to match the pictures.

Cool Squares

Color the squares.

Trace. Draw **2** more squares.

FS109008 • School Skills

Going Home

Draw a line to help each animal find its home.

FS109008 • School Skills

You Need to Finish

Finish the pictures to look like the first one in each row.

FS109008 • School Skills

Yum!

Help Sarah find her cookies.

FS109008 • School Skills

Pick Up Your Socks!

There are **6** socks  hiding in Alex's room. Can you help him find them? Circle them.

Fishing Trip

Connect the dots from **1** to **10**. Color.

14

Let's Count!

Trace and write. Count to **5**.

FS109008 • School Skills

Count and Circle

Circle the correct number in each box.

3   **4**   **2**   **3**

4   **5**   **3**   **4**

Keep on Counting

Trace and write.

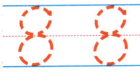

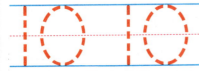

FS109008 • School Skills

Add Some More

Count. Draw more to match. Write the number.

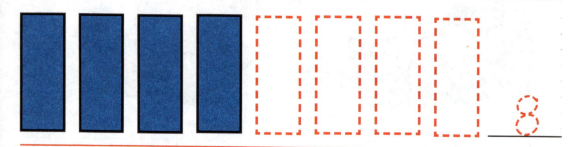

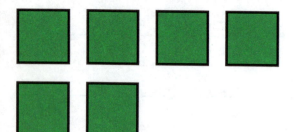

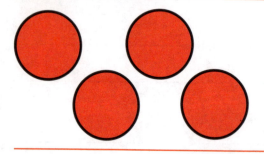

Hear Me Roar!

Connect the dots from **1** to **10**. Color.

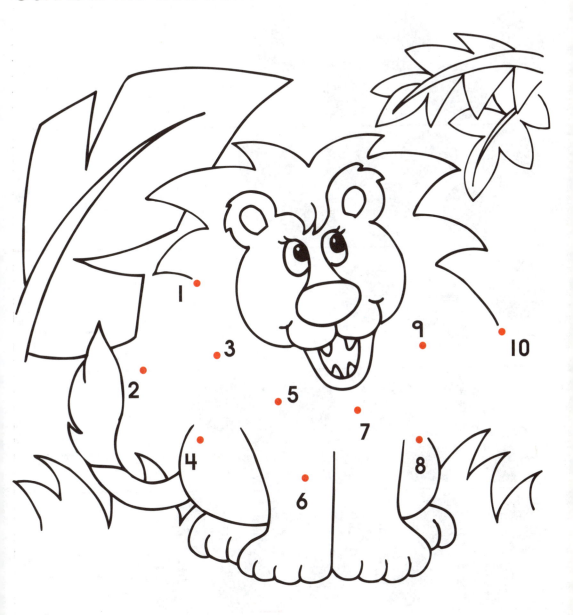

© Carson-Dellosa   FS109008 • School Skills

Perfect Pennies

Count the money. Write the amounts.

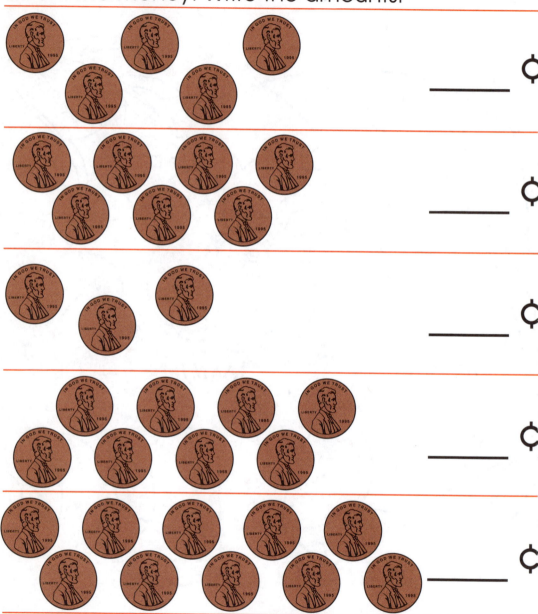

_____ ¢

_____ ¢

_____ ¢

_____ ¢

_____ ¢

FS109008 • School Skills

Count and Color

Color **3**.

Color **6**.

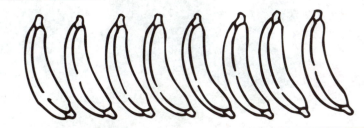

Color **4**.

Color **5**.

Draw **7** oranges. Color **5**.

FS109008 • School Skills

Filling In

Tina is counting her steps. Uh oh! She missed a few numbers. Write in the missing numbers.

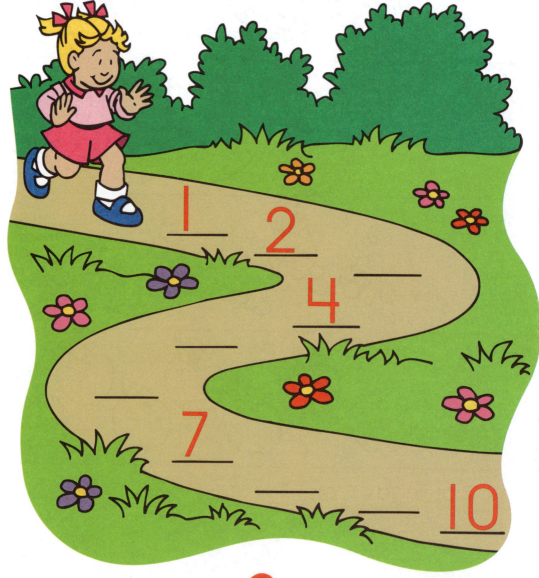

FS109008 • School Skills

Look! Up in the Sky!

Color **4**.

Color **6**.

Color **2**.

Color **7**.

Draw **5** kites. Color **3**.

FS109008 • School Skills

Choosing the Right Color

Trace. Color the things that are **red**.

red

Trace. Color the things that are **blue**.

blue

FS109008 • School Skills

Color Creations

Trace. Color the things that are **yellow**.

yellow

Trace. Color the things that are **green**.

green

FS109008 • School Skills

Choosing More Colors

Trace. Color the things that are **brown**.

brown

Trace. Color the things that are **orange**.

orange

FS109008 • School Skills

Colorful Pictures

Trace. Color the things that are **purple**.

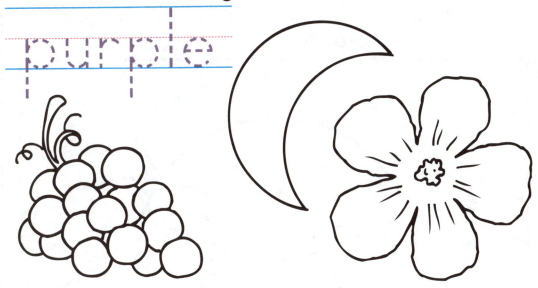

Trace. Color the things that are **black**.

FS109008 • School Skills

Up, Up, and Away

Use the code to color the picture.

1 = **red**   2 = **yellow**   3 = **green**

4 = **brown**   5 = **blue**

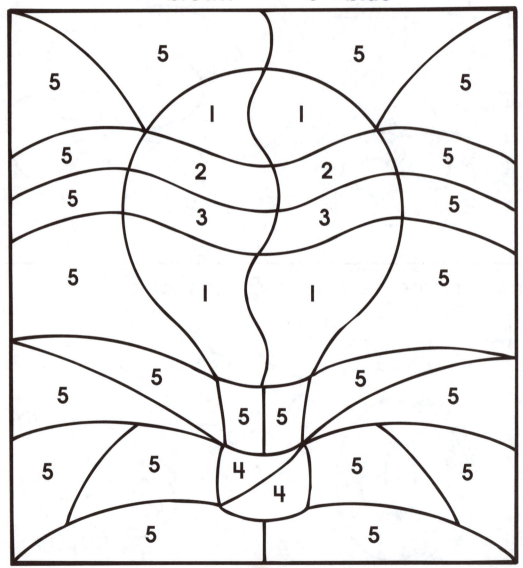

Learning Letters

Trace and write.

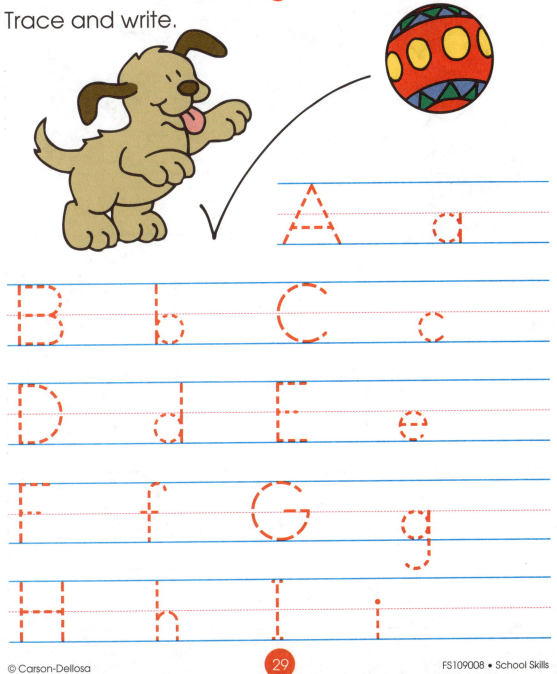

Learning Letters

Trace and write.

Learning Letters

Trace and write.

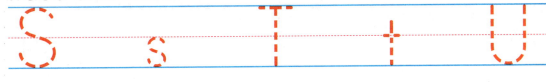

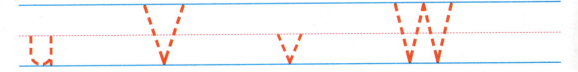

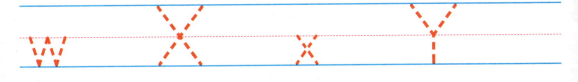

31

Big and Little Matchup

Match the uppercase and lowercase letters.

A	n	E		g
N	a	L		b
Y	y	B		l
I	i	G		e
C	r	J		d
H	c	M		m
R	q	D		j
Q	h	F		f

Which Are the Same?

Color the bees that match the bee on the flower.
Draw a bee to match in the box.

FS109008 • School Skills

A Creature of Long Ago

Connect the dots from **A** to **Z**. Color the picture.

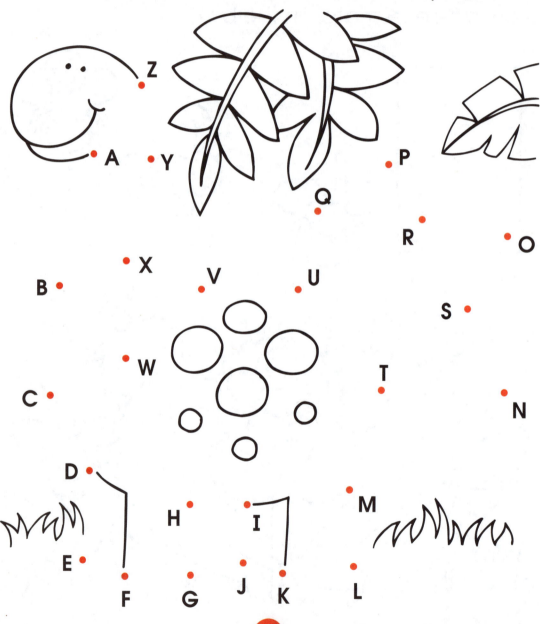

FS109008 • School Skills

Hello, Everyone!

Connect the dots from **a** to **z**. Color the picture.

FS109008 • School Skills

Flying High

Color the things that fly.

 FS109008 • School Skills

I did it!

Amazing Animals

Circle the animal that comes next.

FS109008 • School Skills

Hungry Bunny

Help the bunny find **6** carrots . Color them
orange.

Baskets of Apples

Count the apples in each basket.
Circle and write the number.

6   7   _____

5   6   _____

9   10   _____

6   7   _____

FS109008 • School Skills

Which Is the Smallest?

Color the smallest one in each row.

FS109008 • School Skills

We Go Together

Color the pictures that go together.

Pairs That Match

Color the two objects that are alike in each row.

FS109008 • School Skills

A Super Sound

Color the pictures that start with the same sound as ☀.

FS109008 • School Skills

Mighty M!

Color the pictures that start with the same sound as 🌙.

Bouncing B!

Color the pictures that start with the same sound as .

Circus Fun

Color.

◯ = **red**　　△ = **blue**　　◇ = **green**

Write how many you find.

 _____　　🔴 _____　　🟢 _____

FS109008 • School Skills

Clarence the Clown

Finish drawing the clown to make both sides the same. Color.

FS109008 • School Skills

A Day at the Beach

Find the hidden numbers **1** to **10**. Color them red.
Color the rest of the picture.

FS109008 • School Skills

Match Them Up

Match each picture to its beginning sound.

b

m

s

a

Awesome Animals

Count the animals in each row. Write the numbers.

Hungry Babies

Help the mother bird find her nest to feed her babies.

FS109008 • School Skills

A Fantastic Fruit

Connect the dots from **1** to **10**. Color.

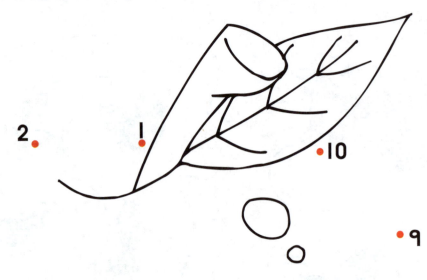

2

1

10

3

9

8

4

7

5

6

FS109008 • School Skills

Happy Hats

Draw a line to match each child to his or her hat.

FS109008 • School Skills

Cheese Chompers

Color the mice that are just like the one in the circle.

FS109008 • School Skills

Love Those Letters!

Write the lowercase letters.

A a B C D

E F G H

I J K L

M N O P

Q R S T

U V W X Y

Z

FS109008 • School Skills

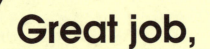
Great job,

_____!

You are ready for school!

signature _____

date _____